Last Warming of the Heart

Poems by
John Murray

Pen Press Publishers Ltd

First published in Great Britain by
Pen Press Publishers Ltd
25 Eastern Place
Brighton
BN2 1GJ

ISBN13: 978-1-906206-21-5

Printed and bound in the UK

A catalogue record of this book is available from
the British Library

Cover design by Jaqueline Abromeit
Illustrations by Alexa Garside

To Jo

Author's Note

Some poems are gifted in dreams, while some are pictures gathered by the wayside. Many are inspired by 'the gentler sex'. Yet others have their origin in recollections and anxieties. This collection includes poems from each of these categories.

A four hundred year old oak tree is pictured on the cover. It stands in my garden, silhouetted against a rock massif, itself 300 million years old, with the timeless Mediterranean Sea beyond.

The great age of the physical world reminds us that our life is short, that the human cast changes constantly and that the hopes and disappointments that preoccupy us will soon count for nothing.

John Murray
Seillans
2007

Contents

The Gentler Sex

Portraits

Reflections

The Gentler Sex

Lara

I am grizzled now and creaking
like an ancient gate, but as she perches
on my arm I feel the memories leaking
from their deep dark store; churches,
baptismal fonts and gowns of lace.

The infant fidgets with my face
besotted with my lower lip,
grasps it in her tiny grip,
the massive bull tamed, a mere twist
of the rope in its nose. Our manly hearts
so easily enslaved, freedom barely missed
in our haste to be adored, Cupid's darts
flying through an open door.

She nuzzles at my ear, more
anguish, my infant daughter reborn
upon my arm.

Italian Girl

She was sitting on a stone
beside a railway track
taking the sun, her black
hair shining, quite alone,
green dress hitched high;
must have been an itching fly
that made her slowly scratch her thigh,
golden-brown rounded perfection;
scornful of detection,
stretching like a cat, insouciante
under the Italian sky.

I carry her with me
this languid lazy girl
in the Po valley.

She

She turns me on.
Nothing special,
no wondrous awe,
no sodden love,
matter of fact
I just like her
to be near me,
breathing her in,
knowing she likes
me close by.

Is this love?
Who knows?
Who cares?

Juliet

I remember a laughing girl,
bright blue eyes through cigarette smoke,
urgent lips, red hair, a curl
adrift upon her nose. We spoke
of poets, of courtly love, the wine
a stimulus to thought; we talked of Donne,
of Mozart, Bach, archangels, fine
conversation, late-night session,
then lapsed into confession
of our love.

No consummation, just her smile.
I didn't see her for a while
and then the phone rang 'just to say
that Juliet has passed away'
at twenty-nine, a crashing car
at two a.m. not far
from home.

I dream of her to tell the truth,
remembering her glowing youth,
her animated gleaming fun,
her predilection for John Donne
and miss her.

Princess

She sat quite still, her cigarette
held as if it mattered, not
just a prop, but essentially her. She let
her profile show. Although a lot
of people dared not look I stole
a glance, but she was ready, staring
me down, coolly amused, the whole
business of attending balls past bearing,
but no mistaking the glance,
seen so often before.

Could I ask her to dance,
dare I take her hand, explore
the surreal unique chance
to waltz round the floor
with a lady of fathomless class?

Alas,
I could not.
I took in her crowd; they had my measure,
lounging back in chairs,
cloaked in insolent stares,
awaiting their princess's pleasure.

Her lovely face frowned that I yet held her gaze,
reality blocking my path, days
in Mustique's sun hardly beckoning.

New Friend

She sidles up, evaluating;
cautious fawn sniffs the air,
watching for movement, waiting,
just out of reach, blonde hair.

I also wait, ready to be there
but mindful of how easily
a deer takes flight I dare not stare
or stretch my hand, breezily
conversing, but tensely aware
of the need for care.

She draws the moon, Selena,
watching now as once she watched
young Phaedra turn from virgin child
towards her fate, incestuous, wild
and doomed.

How will it end
for my little friend?

Old Girl

She smoked her way around the world,
she danced and drank and swirled
her skirts and never ironed her husband's shirts.

Ambassadorial swank her life,
His Excellency's pretty wife,
then he expired and she retired.

The country house was never fun
despite the pool and plants and sun;
all alone in walls of stone

she waited for her children's call,
forever standing in the hall,
the ex-wife counting down her life.

Now they come to feign their sorrow,
loveless, hateful, young. Tomorrow
they will sell the house.

Serious Face

I love her earnest determined frown,
her serious face, when she settles down
to achieve perfection.

I love her primly-tightened lips
when she concentrates, the tips
of hair crossly flicked away.

I love her quiet moods, lashes
lowered while she hides, flashes
of brown when she reveals herself.

I even like the blazing eyes
and the angry way she cries
when her temper flares.

But most of all I love her when
I pin her in my arms, when
powerless she looks into my eyes
and smiles.

Absent Friend

I love her so much
when she is absent
and I can contemplate
in peace the love she
brings to me from
time to time.

Past Her Prime

Bejewelled claws can't hide the flaws,
the too-young hair that bobs and flicks,
the tailored trousers hiding sticks,
the tell-tale chin, too lean and thin,
deserted by her erstwhile youth
her whole ensemble flouting truth.

And yet, she cuts a dash
emanating style and taste,
not short of cash
but gone to waste.

She was a beauty of a sort
but time has caught
her out.

Perhaps someone
still loves her?

Sway

I walked today with two old men,
but spent my time with you.
Haunted by your slender sway,
your smile, your way
of saying nothing but sending
me your quiet glance,
that look, making me want to dance
with you in a never-ending
embrace, your face
close to mine.

A Simple Soul

All parts of you are known to me;
mystery there is none,
not even your profoundest wish.

Soul on sleeve you tread your path
through life, an open book for all
to read and they do.

Artlessness defined, you work
along your well-worn ways,
the modern world disdained

and set at nought, faith
determining your route
to the stars.

But we, the godless,
do not mock you. It's not
as if our modern hell
is turning out so well.

Unrequited

Pleasure has its price,
but I'm willing to pay
for the slow way
she smiles.

The thrill of her arms
will never be mine
but that's fine.
You can't have it all.

My fate to share her charms,
but I don't care,
just to be there,
to see her, is enough.

One day she'll catch
my eye and smile.
Meanwhile
I'll just wait.

The Gentler Sex

They cause a lot of trouble,
fights and disagreements,
barging their way through
life, all attitude and teeth,
their maintenance a fortune.

Dogs and women.
You wonder if you love them.
Then they go
and you know.

Last Holiday

She doesn't want to speak;
company the last thing she desires,
just to be alone in wind and water,
Ophelia without the dying, pretty shells
displacing troubling thoughts.

He doesn't know their names, at least
not more than anyone else. Orion,
the Bear, Arcturus, but he has to stare
nonetheless, sating himself on black
and silver in place of sleep.

There was a time
when they wanted only each other,
but that was long ago.

Skylark

Cover me with my overcoat
and let me dream of long ago.
I promise not to stir.

I will not come to haunt you,
nor will the thunder of war
awaken me.

I will dream of those days
when the world was fresh,
its virgin innocence entire

and you held my hand
and said you loved me,
while the skylark sang.

Portraits

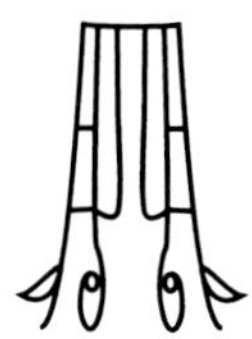

My Friend

We didn't have a lot to say
that day, but we had another drink
while we didn't say it.

He's not so well, my friend,
and if his life should end
before I go, I think
I will remember him that day,
happy, at peace, content to be
there sitting with me
with nothing to say
in the sunshine
beneath the plane trees.

Just us, the wine
and the breeze.

Enemies

They never stop, their discontent
imbuing every minute, dissent
defining their aged union.

Time has leached all feeling of communion
between the weary pair and now their fight
is mortal, bearing down on every issue,
verbal trips and interruptions, spite
evident in their very being, in every tissue.

Measured slurs, well-timed interventions,
contradictions slowing down the stories
making clear the ratified conventions
of their ancient war. His aged glories
vilified, her antique triumphs nullified
by hate and envy. One day they'll lie
in peace, warfare stilled the day they die.

Grand Chap

He seemed a somewhat bumptious sort,
sitting in state, holding court
and later when he spurned my hand
I quietly fumed, looking for a fight,
but it turned out alright;
actually he was a grand
chap.

He was waiting his end
a few months to go, not far
from the finishing line.

We dwelt upon the God of Wine
and finished friends,
but not for long it seems.
Life interrupted by the world of dreams,
so it ends.

Sick, Old and Blind

'Nurse, nurse, NURSE!

Please help me.
Somebody help me, PLEASE!
I'm so frightened.
I want to go home
to my own room.
Fetch me a doctor, please,
I only want to wash
my hands and face
and brush my hair.

Nurse, nurse, NURSE!

Is anyone there?
Will nobody answer me?

Oh dear, I am so frightened.

I want to die.'

Passive

She never bothered leaving
him, all that messy upheaving
and asset-carving, just to escape
his moods, his sagging shape
and bored indifference.

Fiddling with the flowers,
knick-knacks re-arranged,
towels and bedding changed,
her empty hours
passing in dreams of love
before the unseen withering.

His death brought no relief,
piling loneliness on grief
for her wasted life.

Alzheimer's

'He doesn't work here any more.'
Eyeballs roll behind her back,
the little lady dressed in black
wondering if they ever saw
her husband.

'Come on Missus, let's go now,
we'll get you safely on the bus,
no, no, it isn't any fuss,
he won't be coming anyhow,
not today.'

Reluctantly she leaves the school
convinced that they have got it wrong;
he never left her quite this long
and he was going to miss his tea
if he didn't look sharp.

The bus passes the cemetery
but she doesn't remember.

Phryne

If only she could come to life,
spring from the marble and reach
for her cloak, naked shame
relieved. He might have called her wife
but chose to bare her peach-
like skin for all the world to name,
the mistress of Praxitiles.

Talent notwithstanding,
hardly the work of a gentleman.

Faded

She used to be a beauty,
oh, what a beauty,
her lips full and wide
the eyes of a child
and hips that swung as
she walked Bardot-like,
imbued with grace
below her lovely face.

The thickening was not her fault,
we like our girls to bear our young
and hair turns pale as life slips by,
but why
that faltering smile and the look
of puzzled hurt?

Men, imperfect beings, do their thing,
regardless of the pain they bring
and women wait with anxious gaze
hoping for kinder better days.

Piano Singer

Gifted, probably deranged,
singing from her damaged soul
songs arranged
round nursery rhymes,
deadly lines reflecting times
of loss and pain,
embedded in children's tunes.

But don't try to stroke her,
don't think to console her.
She is grief itself
and dangerous.

We won't see her again,
poor mad Nina.

Fall

He lost his footing as he crossed
the kerb, reading the front-page news,
an old man in a cap, lost
in his lonely world of 'whose
mare was dead' this summer day.

He fell slowly without drama
and kept quite still, nobody calmer
than he, blood flowing as he lay
in the road. Rushing to help they came
from every quarter, the butcher's daughter,
a passing gent who immediately sent
for the pompiers, a weeping old dame,
an Englishman who brought a chair,
a neighbour picking up the shopping,
while the old man quietly sat, aware
and stoical, though there was no stopping
the bleeding nose and mouth. I found
his broken glasses on the dusty ground
and slipped them in his pocket. Don't know
why, as he could hardly read through
broken lens, but it made me feel as though
order had been restored.

Widower

Her silky skin haunts him still,
especially in the empty nights
of sleeplessness.

Thank God he chose the fire
and not the writhing worms.

But he hasn't yet
burned her dresses.

He presses
his face against the soft
cotton of her nightgown and weeps.

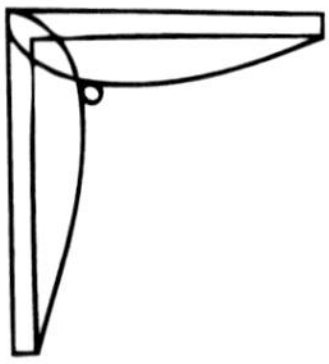

Reflections

Sunset Warning

Sunsets are for the old,
a last warming of the heart
before the bone-deep cold
of unrelenting night.

The young should glance away
lest they take fright
as that last dart
of gold ends the day,
lest their youthful souls be chilled
by sadness as the world is stilled.

At Sea with Belloc

Belloc writing on the sea,
inspiring fugitive dreams
of lonely innocence, his solitary
self-sufficient soul searching
a simpler saner life, sailing
the wilful tides around
his native shore.

No more
do we hear the sound
of distant foghorns in the haar,
the mewing kittiwakes,
or barking seals far
out to sea. The soul awakes
to music such as this,
but no such bliss
awaits us in these grim atonal days.

The orchestra plays
endless fugues on a theme of greed,
while dreams of better days recede
on the ebb tide.

After the War

Soot in the air and in my hair,
gas-lights sputtering as they flare,
cart-horse clopping with its dray,
a post-war schoolboy's end of day.

Exciting to be out at dark
and take the short cut through the park;
we'd walk and say we'd missed the bus
although it made our mother fuss
and warn of dangers,
wicked strangers,
etcetera.

Just a few short years before
I'd seen my grandma clutch the door,
colour draining from her face,
the news from Belgium or some place
was bad. She quickly lost her mind,
like many others of her kind
whose darling son had lost his life,
leaving a shadow of a wife
for poor old grandpa.

I carried on playing conkers,
but didn't much enjoy
being the boy
whose granny was bonkers.

Roots

You can say that you've outgrown all that stuff
of childhood reminiscence, nostalgic dream
of sand and plaits and swimming baths, rough
towels, grit in the air, the puffing steam
trains long since scrapped, just couldn't last,
life has moved on, those days have passed.

You can say that. Fine.

But I am not sure
you're
right.
Quite
suddenly a tune, a scent, a strand
of thought can make us pine
for cycle rides, for coke and coal,
the rubbed-in Vick beneath the vest,
the wash-bowl on my grandpa's chest,
the pears and apples that we stole,
the half-crown present once a year,
the aunts and uncles living near,
her perfume and his smelly pipe
somehow live on, like the stripe
in a stick of rock.

I put them up upon the shelf,
but take them down despite myself.
It may be stupid
but I can't help it.

Village Fete

Seems like a dream of long ago,
the pipes and drums, the whirling skirts,
the pretty bonnets, scarlet shirts,
respectful clapping from the crowd
when it ends.

Seems like a dream of yester-year,
the wide-eyed children in the square,
the pompous bluster of the mayor,
the whiff of grilling in the air,
the smiling friends.

Seems like a dream of distant youth,
my arm encircling a waist,
her hair so silky, lips so near,
murmured words I could barely hear,
the fairground noise, her sweet-faced
charm, but in all truth
I can't recall her name.

Selfish

I hadn't really thought it through,
but now I think I see
that when I said I wanted you
I really wanted me
to be adored and venerated,
waited on, admired and stroked
despite my failings, adulated,
feel my very essence soaked
in constant praise.
Then if there were days
enough to spare
I would care
for you.

Truth

Truth, that ultimate confession
of deep unuttered verities aching
to escape, the final expression
of self, those hard heart-breaking
words, life-changing, is best
left buried in the desert of diurnal
platitudes.

It isn't always wise to show your heart.
I gaze at the setting sun
through a black-limbed tree
and out to sea, memory
sifting what was left undone,
as the final dart
of golden light
kisses day goodnight.

Venus

Up at five, poor night again.
Then Venus nails me, yellow-bright,
a deeply serious light
piercing the duck-egg blue
of dawn. The sulphuric rain
cannot be true.

Uncertain

Slow hardening of the heart as days
shorten; so why these tears?
Nobody's fault, no-one is to blame,
it's just life, an endless game
of closing doors, of new starts,
lonely aching hearts,
wandering lanes, weary ways
to nowhere.

The new moon rises crescent-thin,
the seed lies yearning for the spring,
the timeless rock awaits the sun
and I peer down a sightless road,
uncertain.

Dreams

I sometimes dream of tender girls
who smother me in golden curls
and kiss me gently as I sleep.

And then again I dream of friends
who left us long ago, they send
their love. They wake me and I weep.

I sometimes dream of bounding youth,
my limbs so strong and then the truth
returns as day begins to creep
into my consciousness, so stiff,
so painfully beset by age, as if
my youth had never been.

They hurt, these dreams of distant bliss,
these recollections of a kiss,
those days of glory, dimly seen
and yet there was a time when all
the world seemed there for me, a tall
and potent might-have-been.

My guardian angel came tonight
and warned me that it might
be soon. But that too was a dream.

High Sadness

Mountains chill the soul;
broodingly they wait for prey,
their granite gaze
promising fine-weather days,
their storms concealed
in violet folds, revealed
too late in clouds of lowering grey.

Their moods swiftly changing,
majestic, benign, then ranging
snow seeking out the last warm place
on a freezing rime-encrusted face.

And in the calm late afternoon
they change for dinner, dressing
in their gold and purple gowns
professing harmless beauty.

Don't be fooled.
Mountains are sad
and bad.

Going Mad

I claim the ground between
sanity and madness. I can't explain
the baseless fears, the needless pain
of doubt, the enemy without, unseen
but ceaselessly sensed, never defeated,
his nightly triumphs a repeated
confirmation of derangement.

What happens to the potent mind
cowed by shadows which
itself creates, evanescent dreams rich
in needless terror? One day I'll find
my way back to self-contented
me, lucid, thoughtful, cool and calm,
blessed with wisdom, wit and charm
and cut adrift the poor demented
tenant of my brain.

But then again
I fear he may return.

Dying Adversary

He was once a friend;
it should have hurt much more
to hear that he was near the end,
but long-harboured enmity saw
to that.

Those days of easy friendship long
since gone, viewed through a mist
of hurt and rancour, belong
to another time, a sun-kissed
past.

We must forgive, it is said,
but all I can say
as his life seeps away
in the drug-hushed hospice bed,
is farewell.

Not the Dog's Fault

She is born one freezing morn
on the soil and feels the instant bite
of pitiless dysentery. The light
brings flies and she dies forlorn
and crying.

A few hours old, her story told.

I watch a woman in the park, feeding
birds, using brainless words
to pigeons, ever breeding.

A dog sneaks past, baguette in jaws,
fat, labrador, a thief with paws,
unaware of dying
girls in Africa.

Relinquished Hope

He loved her as best he could.
It wasn't all that good
and she could fairly say
her happy wedding day
was not fulfilled.

Rather as we struggle not to sin
but find the battle just too tough
so their disputes would begin
without malice, then the rough
edge of anger killed

the debate.
Too late
then to sue for peace.
Dull resignation their
only refuge.

Carpe Diem

From warm to cold,
from quick to dead,
a ribbon round the head
to stop
the drop
of the jaw.

Then worms or fire.

So be good, give your love
while you may.
No second chance awaits.

Couldn't Say

I couldn't really say how far away
happiness lies and the same goes for death
and for justice. I roughly know the way
to bliss, a never-ending lover's kiss
and equally I've seen the signs, those lines
which signal passing youth, but as for truth
and justice, I'm not holding my breath.

Relentless years drain away the time,
slow unfastening of our grip on life.
We wander down an unmarked road
to uselessness, until the bell of sickness tolls
and then we live in pain, while our souls
prepare for darkness.

Last Words

I stood beside her dying bed.
'I'm so tired,' she said.
'I just want to sleep forever.'
She never
spoke again.

Too Late

Comes the dawn
and the dead are counted, stiff and grey,
culled at the killing hour of three, they
quietly leave between the night and morn
as wearied daughters steal their missing sleep.

Guilty relief
wrestles with grief
as they straighten the cold
limbs of the old.

'Could you not spend one hour with me? Weep
now, unspoken love finding a voice at last,
now that I am past
caring and deep in sleep.

But I will watch over you, my dearest child,
as the staring
moon watches the earth.'

In the Deep Mid-winter

How far away it seems, the lost ground
of innocence. Fifty years on I still weep,
inconsolable, mourning in the deep
mid-winter of a life run aground
on the rocks of age, childhood
irredeemably gone, the good
left far behind.

An organ winds its ancient threnody around
my head, a monkish medieval sound
of Christmas long ago when pealing
bells proclaimed the Lord was born anew;
the sound of winter, carols stealing
through the freezing streets, through
the frozen icy fields, winding
through the bitter frost
into a small boy's mind,
never to be lost.

Know then Thyself

No-one knows.
Nobody knows those private moments
of inadequacy, those moments
of self-contempt, acknowledgement
that one is not a man
but a hypocritical coward,
incapable of decent generous
self-disregarding humanity,
a living fraud.

No-one knows,
till now.

Dead Tired

Joie de vivre is fine in its place
somewhere at the cutting edge of screaming
fun, but I just want to turn away my face
and start a lethal dreaming.

I am so tired, almost ready now
to discover whether there truly
is an Intelligent Designer, who coolly
worked out how
to stop the water spilling off the earth
when it revolved
and how he solved
the mystery of a virgin birth.

But it doesn't worry me unduly.
I honestly truly
just want to sleep,
turn off the world,
lie tightly curled
and wait for the deep
long silence of eternity.